Dedicated to Mom. I miss you every day.

A special thank you goes to Diane Kane, Jeannine Kries, Barbara Techel, and Erin LeMere.
You ladies helped guide this story to its full potential.

Editor: Rob Daniel

Illustration and Cover Design: Lauren Ackerman

ISBN: 978-1-7339322-2-6

This book or any portion of it, may not be used or reproduced in any manner without written permission except in the case of brief quotations within articles and reviews.

Published In 2020 by Next Voyage Press Wisconsin, USA

Beatrice The Little Camper's Brave New Friend

Written by Lori Helke   Illustrated by Lauren Ackerman

There was so much to do, getting ready for a camping adventure is hard work.

Mr. Tuffle went shopping for yummy campfire treats, and baked chocolate chip cookies to take along.

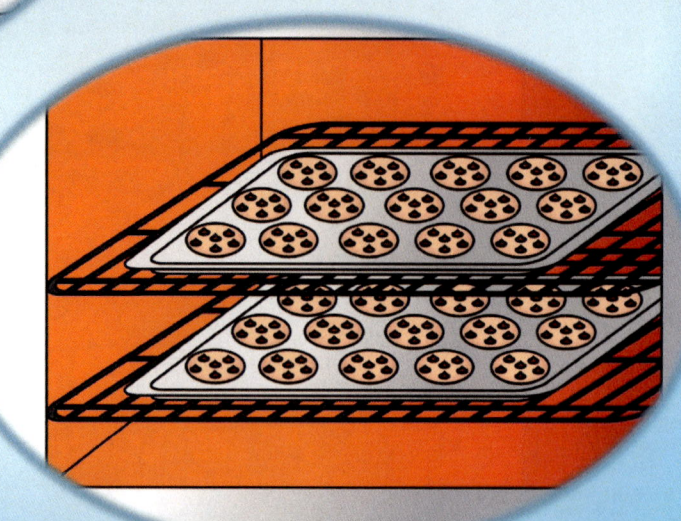

Mrs. Tuffle made sure I was ready for the road.

Ella packed her favorite teddy bear, her butterfly net and magnifying glass.

Zoe made certain Ella didn't forget her food dish and toys.

On the way to the campground, I saw tiny campers that fit only one, to monster campers that can fit a whole football team.

I was hoping to make friends at the campground. What fun that would be, we could play flashlight tag and have a scavenger hunt.

Finally we arrived. As I waited for the Tuffles to get our campsite number, I saw children playing on the playground, heard birds singing in the trees and smelled the campfires. I could taste those s'mores already.

After the camp had been set up, the Tuffles and Zoe left to go swimming in the big lake. That meant it was the perfect time for me to take a nap.

I was exhausted.

Just as I felt myself nodding off, I was jolted awake by the sound of laughter. The three big shiny campers across the road from me were having a great time.

Eager to make new friends, I started to say hi when I realized they were laughing at me. I asked them, "Is something wrong, is my canopy crooked or one of my tires flat?"

Wally, the biggest camper with the fancy gold stripes replied, "No, we're laughing at you because you look different from us. You're shaped funny and very small. You don't belong here, you're too old."

I puffed out my chest and replied confidently. "Of course I belong here, just because I look different to you and am older doesn't matter. I have every right to be here."

Nellie, the camper with the big awning and shiny wheels shouted, "Look around, do you see other funny looking campers like you? This campground is only for big, shiny new campers."

"Go back to where you came from," growled Andy, the smaller camper with the big windows.

I looked but couldn't see any other campers like me. Maybe Wally, Nellie, and Andy were right, and it made me sad to think I didn't belong here.

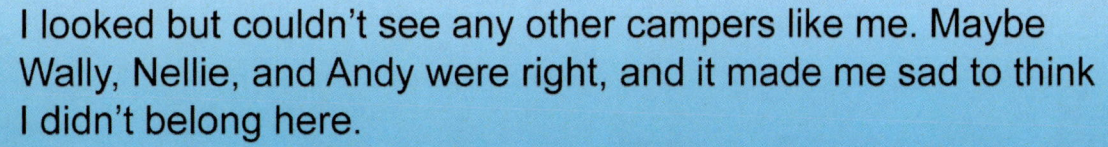

I tried to nap but was too sad. The three campers kept laughing and pointing their fenders at me.

The Tuffles and Zoe returned to the campsite after their swim. While Mr and Mrs. Tuffle built a campfire, Ella and Zoe could see that I was sad.

Ella asked, "Beatrice, are you okay, you look sad?"

"I am sad," I told them. "Those three big campers over there don't like me. They laugh and call me names and say I don't belong here."

A tear appeared in Ella's eye when she said, "Don't let the mean campers get to you. You're special, try to ignore them."

She gave me a hug and Zoe wagged her tail, so I felt a little better.

The next day a fancy red and white camper moved into the open campsite next to me. The Tuffles introduced themselves to the family and offered chocolate chip cookies as a welcome gift.

The Arbor family had a little boy the same age as Ella, and his name was Issac. Ella shared her butterfly net and magnifying glass with Issac and they scampered off to catch butterflies and bugs.

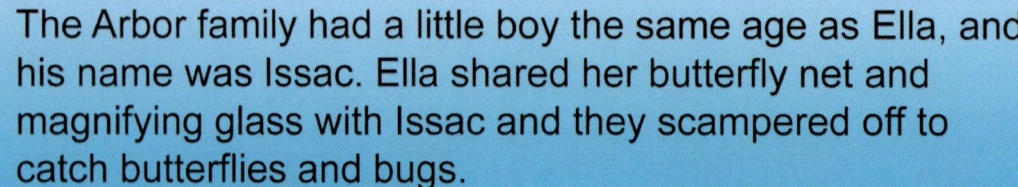

The Arbor's camper was big and shiny like the others, but this one was different. She smiled at me, and this gave me the courage to say shyly, "Hi, my name is Beatrice."

She replied in a friendly voice, which gave me confidence, "Hi, my name is Dolores. It's so nice to meet you.

Dolores and I discovered we liked many of the same things. She loved s'mores and her family, just like I do. She was so nice, and I hadn't laughed this much in ages.

I made a new friend, which was just what I wanted to do.

Dolores and I were having so much fun I didn't notice that Wally, Nellie, and Andy were no longer laughing at me.

When it became dark outside and our families were sitting around the campfire, Dolores and I felt tired so we decided it was time to go to sleep.

An hour later I awoke to the sound of whispers. I opened one eye to see Wally talking to Dolores, and he was telling Dolores she shouldn't be friends with me.

Dolores asked him, "Why not? Beatrice is nice and I really like her."

Wally explained, "But she isn't like us. She's old and she's shaped funny. She's different."

"Just because Beatrice looks different from us isn't a reason not to like her. Maybe if you give her a chance and get to know her, you'll realize she's not so different after all," Dolores replied to Wally.

I felt a tear trickle down my face. Dolores really is my friend, I thought. She's sticking up for me and helping Wally see that I'm a nice little camper.

That night I dreamed about big campers and Dolores. I thought about campers judging other campers just because they looked different. I wondered, "Have I done the same thing as Wally, Nellie, and Andy to another camper? I hope not."

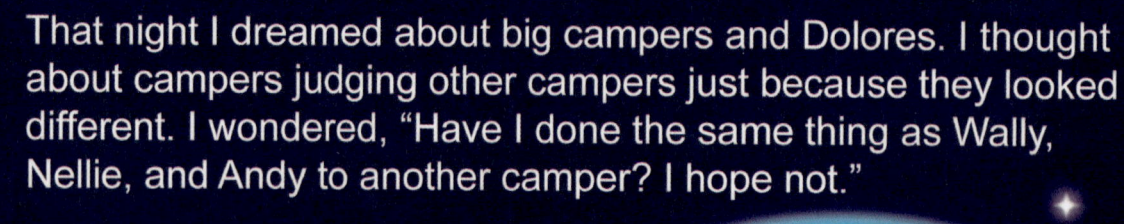

The next morning, I woke up to see Dolores was already awake. She smiled. "Good morning sleepyhead, I have a surprise for you," she said excitedly.

Just then Wally, Nellie and Andy called out together, "We're sorry Beatrice!"

"We were wrong to be mean to you, it wasn't nice," Wally said.

Nellie chimed in, "Dolores helped us see that even though you're different from us on the outside, inside we're all pretty much the same. We like s'mores and our families too."

I looked at Dolores, feeling grateful. "Thank you," I said. "I've never had a friend like you, Dolores. I think we'll be friends forever."

On our last night at the campground, Dolores and I, along with the Arbors and Tuffles, sat by the campfire celebrating new friendships, our differences, and of course, s'mores. What a great camping adventure this had been.

The next day we had to say our goodbyes to the Arbors and Dolores. Ella told me we'd be camping with them again soon. Yippee!

As we drove away Wally, Nellie, and Andy called out "Goodbye Beatrice, Safe Travels!"

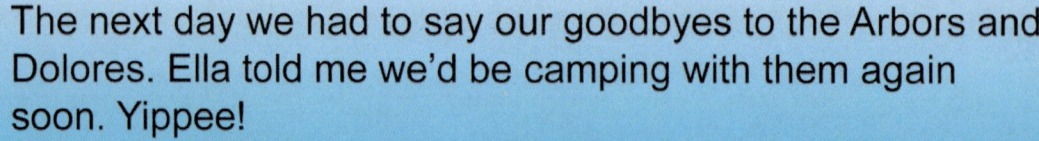

That night when I was safely back at home, I thought about the lesson Dolores taught - not only to Wally, Nellie, and Andy - but me as well. It doesn't matter how different we look, we should always be kind to each other. Treating others with kindness makes us feel all warm and fuzzy inside ...

Like a cozy campfire on a chilly night.

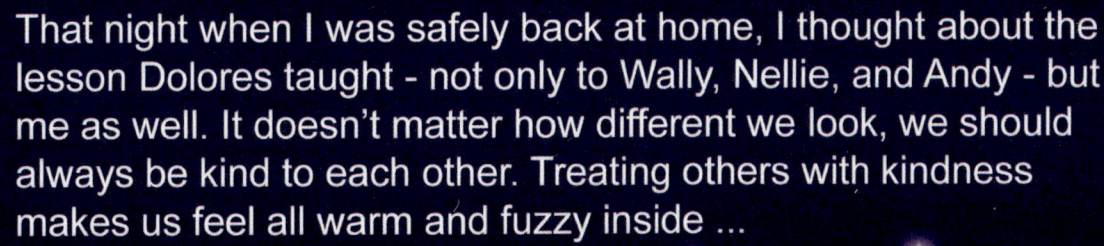

About the Author

Lori Helke lives in Kiel, Wisconsin where she spends time planning adventures in her vintage camper, the real life Beatrice. *Beatrice The Little Camper's Brave New Friend* is the second book in the Beatrice The Little Camper series. She loves Paris, reading, kayaking, and taking her dog Zoe for long walks.

For a free downloadable Parent/Teacher discussion guide, go to lorihelke.com

Connect with Lori Helke

Facebook @lorihelkeauthor

Instagram @beatricethelittlecamper and @lorilovesparis

Author website: lorihelke.com

Twitter @lorilovesparis

Made in the USA
Middletown, DE
22 March 2021